Dear

From one
strong woman
to another,
our strength
unites us.

Love,

Maria B.

SCAR CITY

A POETRY MEMOIR

By

Renaria B.

Tellwell Talent
www.tellwell.ca

ISBN
978-0-2288-2718-4 (Hardcover)
978-0-2288-2717-7 (Paperback)
978-0-2288-2719-1 (eBook)

Table of Contents

Part 4
Healing

Preface

This is a poetic account of some of my life experiences.

Between the ages of 15 and 22 (1990 to 1998), I experienced some severe trauma in my life and multiple hospitalizations.

This book was written as I re-lived and processed these experiences throughout the years. Some of my poems are based on close relationships (*F U*); others are about acquaintances (*Thunder*); and some are about my experiences in the hospital (*Drugs, Benzo Tango*).

Finally, in December 2019, I concluded that forgiveness of oneself is the key to finding solace in difficult times, no matter how long this may take.

This book of poems is a manifestation of my cathartic journey to peace within. My hope is that you can find true happiness too, even in the face of difficult or challenging times.

No matter how isolated or alone we may feel, in the end we have our bravery, our strength and ourselves.

And each other.

We have each other.

And our stories.

Introduction:

The Truth Is In The Scars

I had it all
So figured out
What the scars
Were all about

Through dirty blue
Secrets of you
The pain felt new
Path torn askew

Truth hard to find
As it lay behind
The dark unkind
Gates of my mind

One day I spoke
Kind words of hope
They danced between
My restless dreams

Their silent screams
No longer wild
Somehow forgiven
By my inner child

I wish I knew
When it all came out
I'd have it all
So figured out

PART
1

TRAUMA

(1990-1998)

Cherry Bomb (The First 'Hit And Run')

You were the one
I chose
All of sixteen
And grandiose

You were too eager
I suppose
To rip off
My work clothes

What is it about me?
I wondered shyly
I was nothing
But a baby

Blinded by
Your tenacity
Still your allure
Was my candy

No first date
No romance
No slow dance
Just a foolish plan

So you led me
To a party
Just to hurt me
And then leave me

All of that pain
And no victory
After I cried,
I was empty

So you swayed me
Once again
Though I was still
On the mend

Was it so easy
To pretend?
All you wanted
Was the end

Another grand
Forceful entry
Why can't you see?
You deceived me

Only to leave me
Just as dirty
As my sweet cherry
On the bedsheet

F U (The Boyfriend)

I was 15 when I met you
All I had were
Broken dreams
And a curfew
You tried to take my virtue
I wouldn't let you

I was 18 when I had you
You took me camping
So I let you
I was your girl
I wish I knew
It was too good
To be true

I was 19 when I lost you
You took it from me
When I had the flu
You wanted me
So I thought I had to
My mistake
What about you
What's your
Damned excuse?

I was 15 when I met you
And now I see
The real you
I didn't know it then
It was so new
But there were
Always two of you

Snuffing out my light
With your knife
So shiny and new
Now I really see you
Clearly
Right through
I'm not the same girl
You loved to use

Driving in my car
Suicidal thoughts
Sang what to do
As I flipped over
The cassette of
Tragic love songs
Side one
Side two

Since that day
I grew up
And got a clue
Now I'm enjoying
A much better view
I guess it wasn't
Up to you
Who knew?

I was 15 when I met you
That's why this poem
Isn't about *you*
I won't let you have that
We both know
All this is true

Cause now I can see it too
The rapist in your eyes
Can you?
Yes ... I just wish I knew then
What to do
That's why
This is simply called
F U

Thunder (The Acquaintance)

I thought of that day
When I tried to run away
You grabbed and you pawed
Till I was filthy and raw

While under the weather
I searched hard for shelter
I refused to conform
With my own desperate storm

You followed me home
Where I never felt safe
I picked a few flowers
Under your silent gaze

I looked out my window
You were there, same M.O.
I shook when I saw you
Downed one more benzo

Two years, they went by
My heart nearly died
I couldn't comprehend
Your need to see me again

There was no one to save me
Not sure if any tried
I looked down the road
All my tears had run dry

I waited for you
As you turned to go back
Didn't know what to do
So I planned my attack

I picked up my phone
And grabbed my house keys
I clutched them too hard
Mace keychain handy

I stomped on my garden
Letting go of the burden
I stalked you back, fair is fair
With zero fucks left to care

Have You Ever (Miscellaneous Violence)

Have you ever lost your power?
Reliving scenes of the last hour
Cowering naked in the shower
In dirty tears and bloody water

Have you ever wished the enemy,
Ignored the shame in your dignity?
Always yearning to feel whole
Like the puzzle pieces of your soul

Have you ever longed for kindness,
And found that love is a blindness?
If the visions are your senses
Why's your spirit so defenceless?

Have you ever been the one,
Always chosen to get none?
In the darkness behind the sun
Lies the violence that made you run

Have you ever nursed your wounds?
Black and blue is nothing new
Scared and curled up on the floor
Your swollen eye on the locked door

Have you ever been confined?
Popping pills to pay the fine
Wishing anyone would find
The crime scene they left behind

Have you ever danced with danger?
Made smaller by a stranger's anger
Left to purge it all out after
Have you ever?
Have you ever?

Random Thoughts From The Psych Ward #1
(1995-1997)

~I am a prisoner
A slave
To my past
And my shame

~Are you afraid
Of my potential?
Is it the goodness
Or the evil
Part of me
That makes you
So blind to see?

PART
2

COPING

Benzo Tango

Awakened worry
Creeps in my sleep
Ativan in my hand
With the secrets I keep

You dance in my mind
Sometimes quick
Sometimes slow
The beats are unkind
Like tempo vertigo

Still trapped by the fire
Of my thought inferno
For the calming desire
Of the benzo tango

ADHD And Me

My mental acuity
It seems
Just might
Not be

To think it
Like I see
My lonely
Mind disease

I search for words
I process
I envy
Normalcy

Stimulants
Are clear to me
Soothingly
Necessary

My thought
Capacity
Such jumbled
Ecstasy

My deep
Priorities
To ride the windy
Breeze

I write for sweet
Release
Ponder with such
Great ease

Forget this
Fuckery
It's three and I need
To sleep

Club Med

Lost in a skinny dream
One morning I swallowed a scream
With the darkness its only charm
In a hospital bed on the ward

I ate and ate and ate
Gained a quarter-pound a day
Furious sadness close at bay
Happy pills sitting on the tray

Ninety days on total lockdown
Seldom visitors to be found
No sharp objects and many wrists bound
Just us crazies hanging around

Mood Monster

The beaming night
With no sleep in sight
Faded into dreaded
Darkened daylight

So I then welcomed
The soul's sad lonesome
Happy medium
Dirty Lithium

Such creative fuel
A bipolar's jewel
But it wasn't my call
Enter, Epival

Then I stood too tall
Bouncing off the walls
Couldn't ignore the fall
Hello Risperdal

Now to numb the screams
Of low self-esteem
Through my vivid dreams
Came Olanzapine

Still I could not win
Needed peace within
If thou shall not sin
Guess it's Neurontin

Oh it's just a spell
Yes, you can be well
And no one can tell
With this Seroquel

Are you still in denial?
No, no I'm just fine
Oh okay, then it's time
For Abilify

Yes, I damn well tried
To shamelessly be
What you wanted to see
Simply uncrazy

Hiding all the lows
Killing all the highs
Yet I just long to cry
One more lonely time

Drugs

You pick me up
Or calm me down
You help me sleep
And level me out
You set me straight
Or set me back
Dreams obsolete
Keep me on track
I am what I am
You see what you see
At least I am high
If I can't be me

Random Thoughts From The Psych Ward #2
(1995-1997)

~Colour my skin
In bright shades
So someone
Will notice me

~The thoughts of death
Are present
Of course
But to mutilate my body
Is a stronger
Infatuation
Because I am trying
To tear off the flesh
That is hiding the light
That this demon
Called depression
Has taken
From me

~My life is controlled
By routine
And stability
But I feel
The need
To be wild
Disorganized
And irresponsible
Who am I?
Why am I here?
What does
Everyone
Expect from me?

PART
3

PROCESSING

The Days Of Nothing

When the song in your heart is silent
And your tears show through your soul
Drink from the spirit of your island
Isolated in your self-control

As you dig through words of longing
Search for the love you crave
Those are the days of nothing
No armour in the arms of the wave

Flee from the shells you hide in
You will find the truth, beware
Love the scar—it guides you
Naked as you are, it ends there

I Digress

I don't like pain
Yet I know it well
It's a curse from hell
I can't dispel
Should I wear it like a glove?
Or hide it well?
It doesn't even matter
Most of you
Can't tell

I feel like love
Forgot me
Along the way
Instead of holding on to it
I just gave it all
Away

Yet I can't hide my sadness
It lurks in my madness
Behind a face
That should care less
About the masses
And the business
Of assaulting me
With fake kindness

What the fuck?
Is this nonsense
I'm done
Smelling roses
And doing poses
From now on
It's bleeding noses

Okay
There I said it
What's your definition,
... of tragic?
If I laugh out loud
Am I manic?
Or in the magic
Of the static?

No I don't like pain
Yet I know it well
But as far
As I can tell
You can aim
To get well
Wind up dead
Or in a cell
Whether you get this or not
This to you
I swear
If you see me
Out there

Beware

I still care

Secrets We Share

Do you feel me?
See my truth?
I hide behind
My crazy mind
Yet you still judge
What I've
Been through

I don't mind
If your concern
Is to learn
How I yearn
To return
From the gash
Of the senseless lash

Cause if you care
Enough to share
That you, too
Have been there
Then you should know
To hold your own
And not compare
This secret prayer

My soul's now renewed
But yet you still shoot
Right through the target
Of my point of view

Now I'm awake
Make no mistake
I can relate
I know the hate

Just be aware
The world's not fair
There is enough
Despair to share

Random Thoughts From The Psych Ward #3
(1995-1997)

~I want to be forgiven
To be free
But they do not feel
The scar
That is burning
Within me

~Who are we to judge
The decency
Of our own selves?
The status
We believe
We fit
So securely
Will we ever
Live up
To the standards
In which we are
So dearly
Committed to?

PART
4

HEALING

Moving Forward, Facing Back

I crawled up from under
My painful protector
The sky was so bright
I was crippled with fright
At ease with the night
How I feared the daylight

Way under the rock
Lay secrets that I thought
Too guarded to abort
Locked and loaded, in their vault

It begged me to come back
Like an old friend might ask
Said, 'it's not an attack
Let me rest on your back'
So much more left to stack
Behind the beauty and the mask
Slipping out through the cracks
Black tears, facing facts

I dug through the dirt
Found earth and old hurt
It wasn't as surprising
As the burden of dying

I sensed new beginning
My hope was ascending
I stopped
My jaw dropped
The truth
It was raw
I just saw
What I saw
Oh this place
Yes it was
Just as lonely
Just as sorry
As my rock
And my story

Forgive Me

I was only as damaged and weak
As I allowed myself to be
The shame and guilt I'd see
Was abuse, caressed by me

There was nothing more to see
Than my foolish consistency
As the pain inside of me
Was screaming to be set free

I didn't know it could be
As simple as saying, 'I'm sorry'
To myself, damaged and weak
Yes, the power ... it lay within me

The Final Cut

I was a victim in my mind
Played like a fool by you
For years I self-abused
Swift motions, clean and new

The chains you loosened slowly
As you nurtured my demise
My pain guarded me softly
Bandaged shame, close by my side

The blade was sometimes dull
As darkened days might be
Red lines so comfortable
Never drawn for you to see

One day I spoke a word
It echoed deep and true
My scars had never heard
My voice so free of you

Random Thoughts From The Psych Ward #4 (1995-1997)

~Can you take me away
From all
This misery
And doubt
Or do I stand alone
In all
That my thoughts
Are about
Meet me halfway
I'm waiting
Undress my skin
And tell my soul
That I will not
Let evil win

~Fate is the hand
Life gives you
And destiny
Is what you do
With that hand

Storm

Although it wasn't
My design
It was a storm
And it was mine

I pray sometime
I'll leave behind
Sad moans I've owned
Hurt rarely shown

For years I coped
Bled tears of hope
Only to find
Pain reassigned

I hid from rain
Guarded the stains
Warm rays maintained
What I'd restrained

It was not kind
Nor my design
It was a storm
And it was mine

Biography:

Renaria B. lives in Toronto with her husband and her Devon Rex cat.

Book Description:

Have you ever longed for kindness, and found that love is a blindness...?

Powerfully explicit and beautifully crafted, SCAR CITY is the raw personal journal of one woman's path to self-forgiveness amidst the chaos of an unruly mind.

Special thanks to:

First and foremost, I would like to thank my husband, aka the oracle, for being the brightest star in my life. Thank you for respecting the pain and the process, but most of all, for your love and constant source of light during all those inevitable dark days.

Lindsay: For the years of support, the ideas, the friendship and for always believing in me.

Francis: For the friendship, the interest, and willingness to discuss dark subjects. And for suggesting to print.

Andy: For reading every poem as they were written and the constructive feedback.

Dad: For passing on your love of words, passion for equality and respect for the human condition.

Opale: For the unconditional love and honesty.

Thank you to those who contributed:

The illustrator (who wishes to remain anonymous). For the creative vision and for being present. You have the gift of transforming emotion into art. You are truly talented and appreciated.

Jamie and Lisa: For the photography and for focusing so much of your time on my wellbeing, especially throughout this project.

Matty: For the shoulder to lean on, the artistic direction and the hair skills.

Mitchell: For the empathy, patience and understanding at any hour, day or night.

To my early readers, thank you:

Vee
Phil
Michèle
Tasha
Simone

CPSIA information can be obtained
at www.ICGtesting.com
Printed in the USA
BVHW061201270620
582418BV00012B/211/J

9 780228 827184